EMOTIONS
IN LETTERS AND ART

Letters of Joy

Mariia Biriukova

HAPPINESS AND GRATITUDE

Letters of Joy

A Creative Journey of Hand-Lettering, Coloring, and Self-Expression
© 2024 by Special Art

All rights reserved. No part of this publication may be reproduced, distributed, or transmitted in any form or by any means, including photocopying, recording, or other electronic or mechanical methods, without the prior written permission of the publisher, except for brief quotations in reviews or non-commercial uses permitted by copyright law.

For permissions, contact: support@specialartbooks.com

Published by Special Art Books | www.specialartbooks.com

Paperback ISBN: 9791255531890

Images © Shutterstock

This book belongs to

....

4

TABLE OF CONTENTS

★ Introduction...6

★ Rhythm and Pattern....................................... 8

★ Basics of Lettering..12

★ Lettering Practice..16

★ Gratitude Postcards..................................... 54

★ Happy Word Cloud......................................84

★ Reflection and Celebration.............................. 102

INTRODUCTION

Welcome to *Letters of Joy*! Discover and celebrate the joy within you by embarking on this beautiful journey of calligraphy and lettering. Be enlightened through the therapeutic and uplifting practice of digging deep into your experiences and expressing joy, sharing joy, and becoming more joyful.

Calligraphy and lettering are more than just art forms — each stroke can be used as a tool for emotional expression. Through this book, you will learn to unlock feelings of happiness and contentment. The results of your creative activities will be your beacons of light and will remind you and others to live a life filled with joy.

Why does joy matter in life and in lettering? There is an inherent feeling of accomplishment whenever a person creates art. There is an even greater feeling of joy when that art brings a smile to someone special. In your life, you have experienced many ups and downs. In the moments that you've responded with joy, you glow and emanate that same feeling to the people around you.

Joy is contagious. So when you're lettering, the joy you have also passes on to the art you are creating. In this book, you will learn new techniques in lettering and create different projects through practical exercises, all while being mindful and deepening your understanding of joy.

As you turn the pages, let the joy of letters unfold. Discover the happiness that comes from creating something beautiful with your own hands. Remember, this journey is about more than just learning a skill—it's about finding joy in the process and sharing that joy with others. Welcome to *Letters of Joy*.

TOOLS YOU WILL NEED

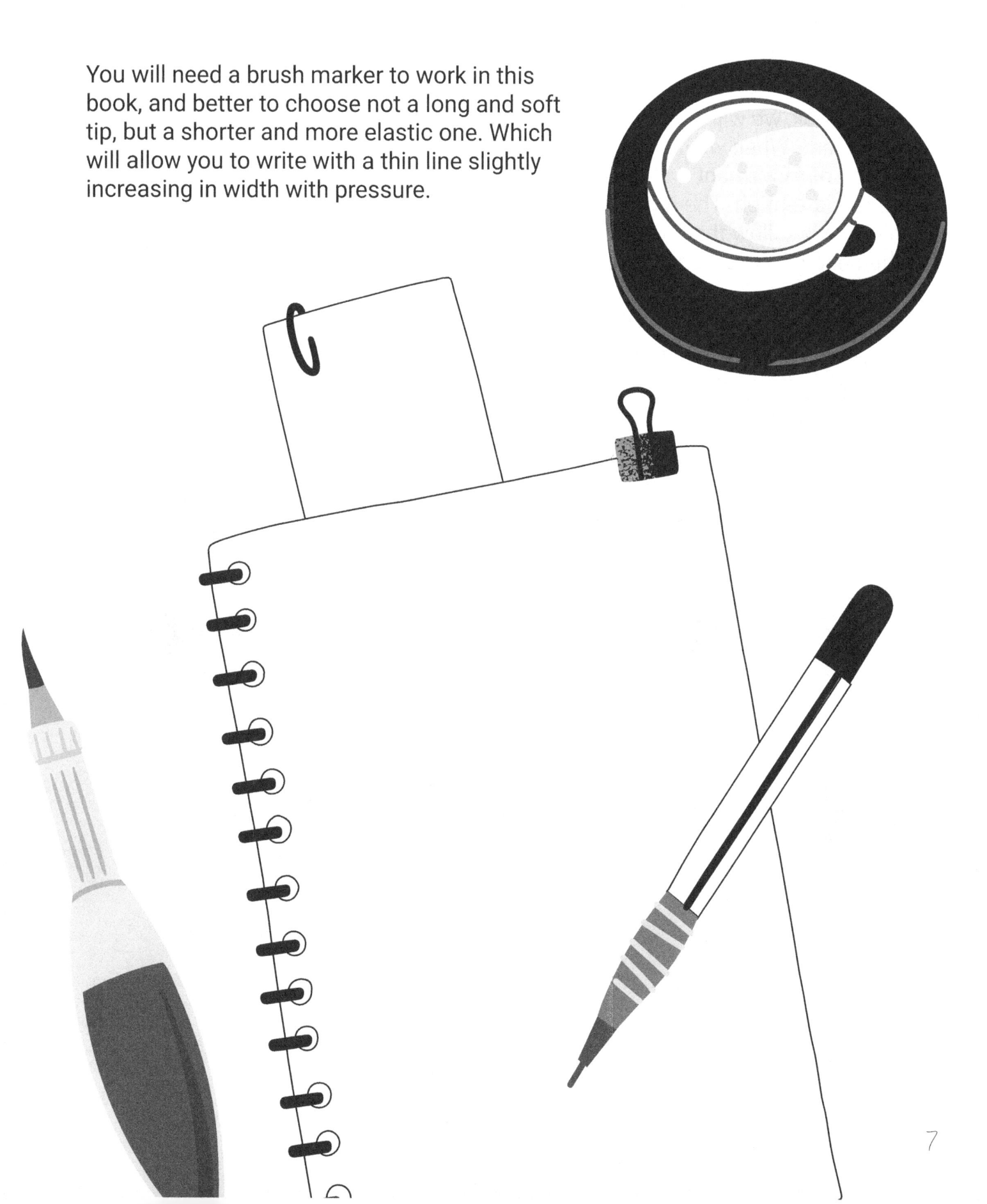

You will need a brush marker to work in this book, and better to choose not a long and soft tip, but a shorter and more elastic one. Which will allow you to write with a thin line slightly increasing in width with pressure.

RHYTHM AND PATTERN

In this book, we will look at rhythm as a way of creating movement. When we see a rhythmic pattern, an optical illusion of movement and flow is created and this always attracts attention. The movement of the viewer's attention will always follow the rhythms in the artwork. Rhythm occurs when one or more elements are repeated, as in music.

To create a rhythm, you need to organize a composition of objects that repeat over and over again - lines, spots, or their features - size, shape, texture.
It is important to keep in mind the visual weight of each element and how they work together.

Let's see how this works in practice! Follow the grid to create rhythmic patterns.

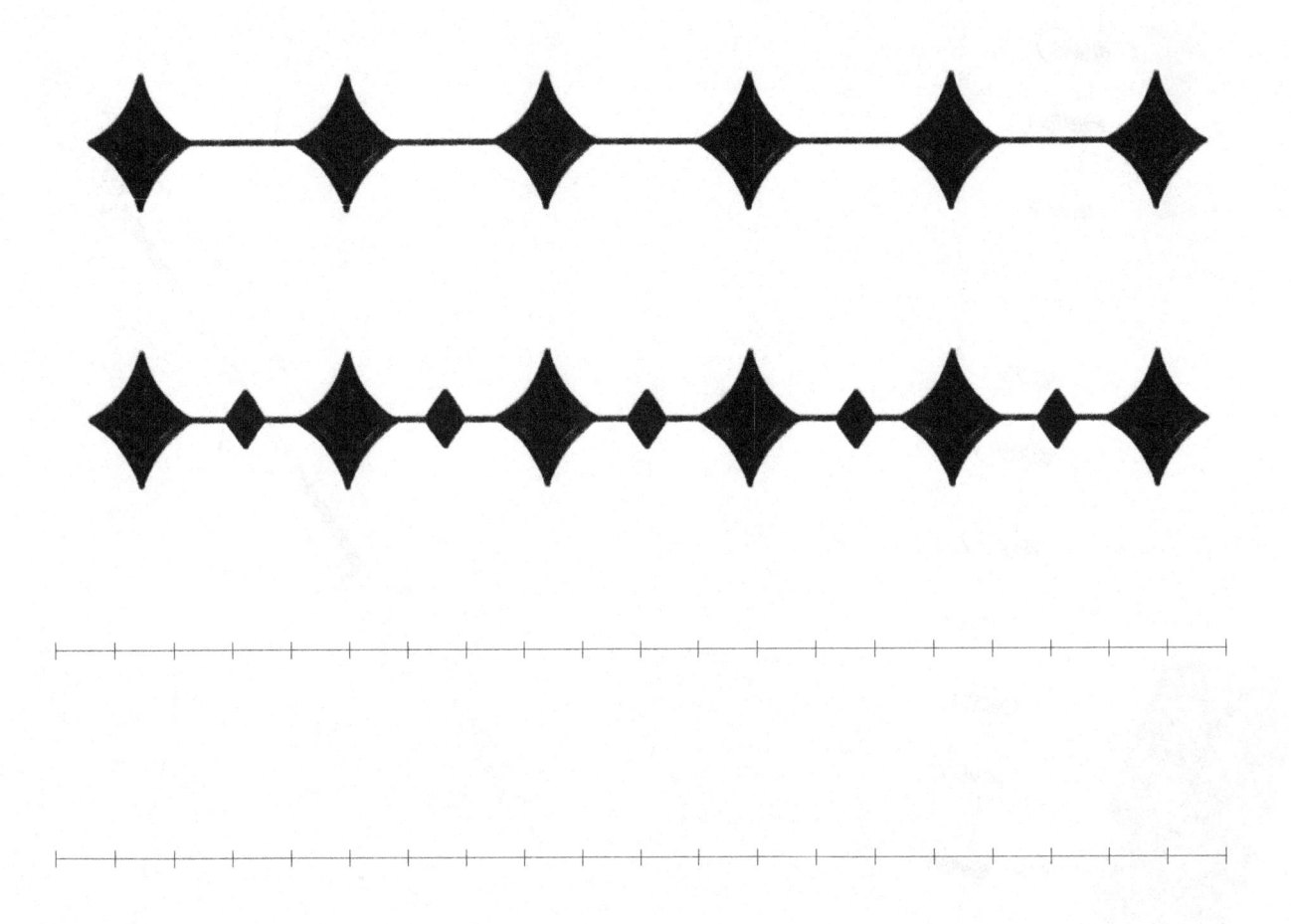

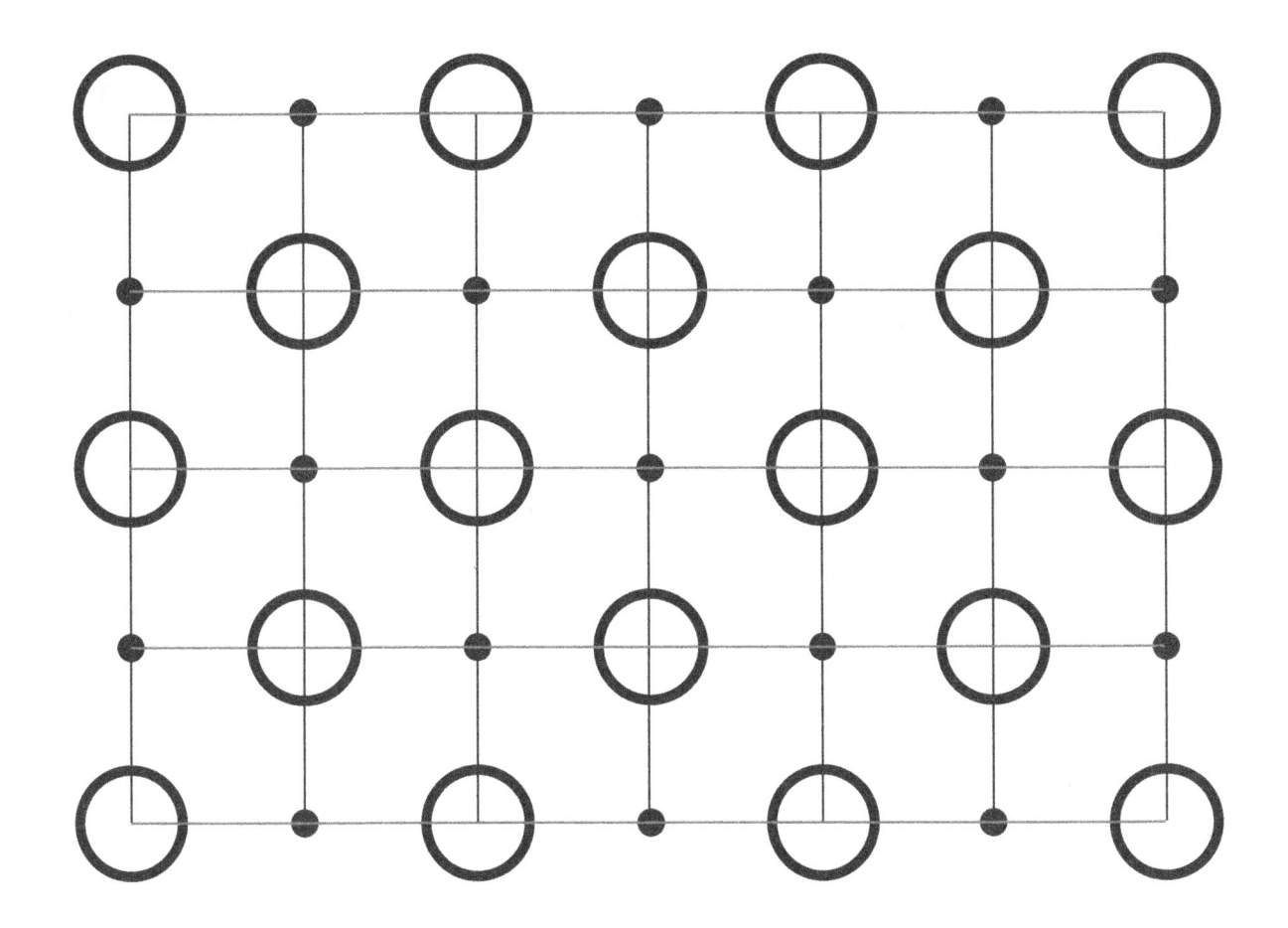

Place the repeating elements on the grid.

10

When objects gradually get smaller — it creates the illusion of perspective. This is a good example of how hierarchy is built within a composition. Therefore, when creating a composition, it is always important to correctly balance what is important and what is secondary.

Letters are also made up of repeating elements. And these elements create rhythm and flow, which makes it easy for us to read. But if we want to add a visual impact and create an atmosphere, we can increase the rhythm or break the rhythm to attract attention.

BASICS
OF LETTERING

Whether you're new to this art form or seeking to refine your skills, going through the foundational strokes is always a good way to warm up your writing muscles.

In this chapter, you'll start with two of the basic strokes in lettering: the upstroke and down stroke. Remember that how hard you press your pen on the paper makes the difference in how the strokes look. For the upstroke, it should be thin using light pressure, while the down stroke is thick and requires heavier pressure on the paper.

The rhythmic movement of your pen will not only help you develop precision and control but also bring a sense of calm and focus. Grab your favorite brushpen and let's begin with the first exercise!

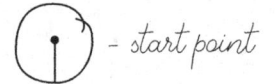

- writing tool (brushpen)   - start point   - line direction

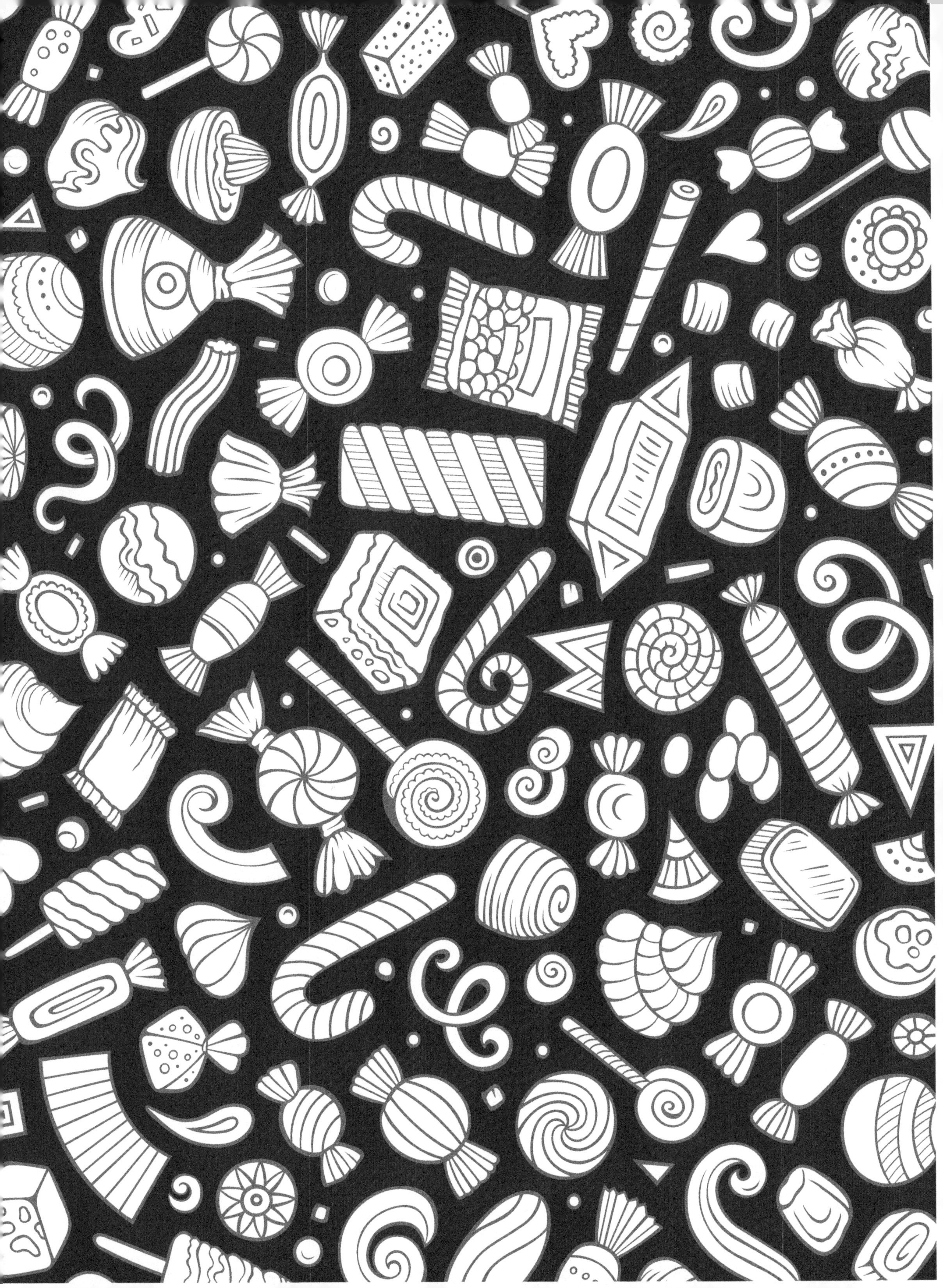

Use this space for more practice. Every great letter starts with a single stroke!

LETTERING
PRACTICE — *color it*

Joy can look very different from person to person. It can be loud and fun but also peaceful and calm. It depends on how you express this emotion and how you respond to what's happening around you.

In the next few pages, you'll start learning new styles of lettering. You will practice loops and flourishes and combining these letters to form beautiful words. Remember to use what you've learned about rhythm and movement.

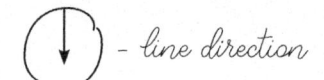

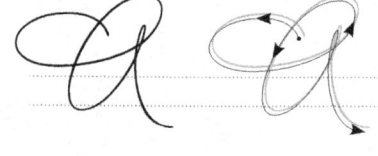

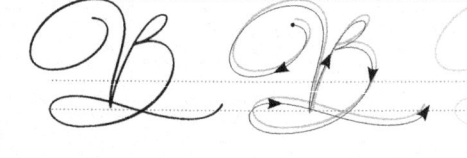

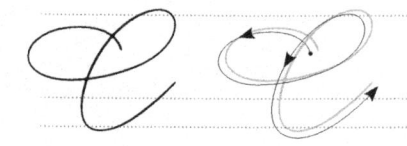

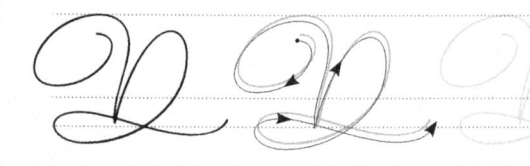

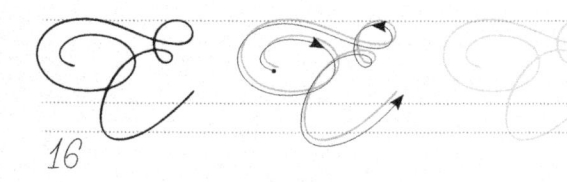

- *writing tool (brushpen)*
- *first line*
- *line direction*

color it

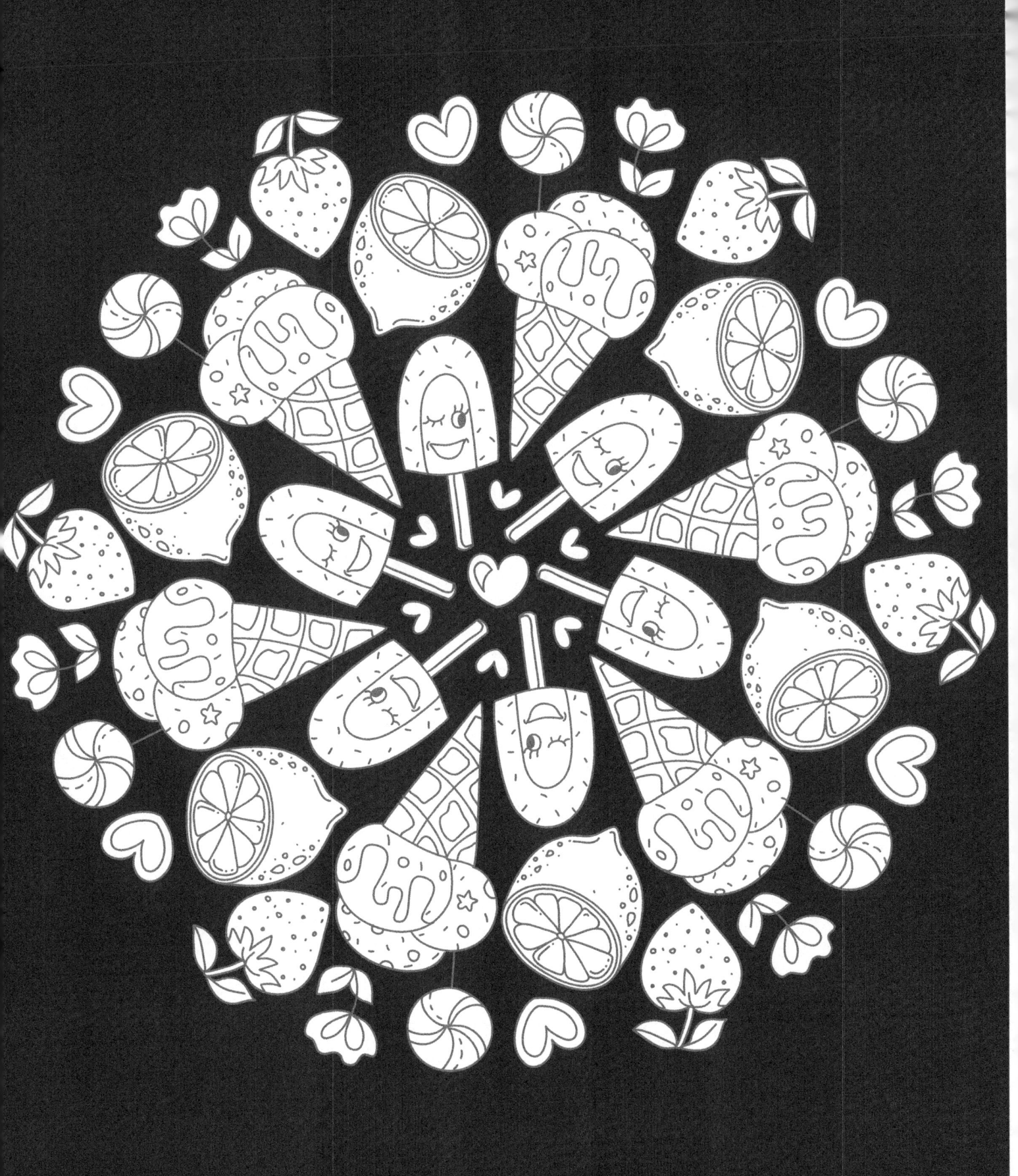

When you're engaging in repetitive strokes, it forces your mind to focus and be mindful. This exercise helps you be more present and in the moment. It also helps you recognize your emotions and express those emotions through lettering.

Did you notice? The letters in this exercise use a consistent pressure instead of a thicker down stroke. In lettering, creative expression is highly encouraged. The beauty in this art form is that there will always be something new to learn. Just like in life!

Choose joy even on the grayest of days

Seeing your skills improve over time can boost your confidence. With every stroke you make in these exercises, you are getting closer to adding a new skill to your toolkit.

Let's now move to practice the lowercase letters of this style. Lowercase letters provide a certain rhythm when writing. It shows how everything — even simple things — can be important. Remember to celebrate small wins.

Let your heart dance to the rhythm of joy

People manifest joy differently. How do you show your joy? Do you find yourself smiling a lot? Do you talk about what made you joyful to your closest friends? Think about all the ways you show joy to yourself and the people around you.

As you continue this exercise, be mindful of how you're holding your writing instrument. Are you gripping it too hard? How is your posture when sitting? Are you tensely positioned over your work? Take some time to stretch and relax your shoulders.

Happiness blooms from within.

When you've finished practicing this lettering style, take a separate piece of paper and use what you've just learned to write some words of encouragement. You can even practice with writing your name in this style first.

We will now start with a new lettering style. For the next few pages, you will need to use a little more pressure on the down strokes to accentuate the letters. The flourishes in each letter flow from thick to thin, so be mindful and focus on the movements.

- writing tool (brushpen)   - first line   - line direction

Chase the moments that make your heart smile

Happiness is usually a response to something that happens in someone's life. Joy, on the other hand, is an emotional state that can be more lasting than happiness. Joy is not dependent on the circumstances around you, but can be enhanced by your gratefulness.

These playful letters can be used as display letters for banners and headings. You will notice this style in shop signs and anything that needs to catch attention. When you rest after these exercises, try and look around to see similar styles around your neighborhood.

Find joy in the little things for they make up the big moments.

What are you grateful for today? Being more aware of the things that make you grateful increases the joy in your life. It doesn't have to be a big event. You can even be grateful that you've finished practicing the capital letters of this style! Think about other things that make you grateful today.

The lowercase letters of this style have less flourishes. You may notice that it is similar to the usual cursive writing that is taught in schools. The difference is still in the added pressure on the down strokes. The pressure you add to the letters gives it the distinct style.

a a a a

b b b b

c c c c

d d d d

e e e e

f f f f

g g g g

Your smile is the sunshine that brightens even the cloudiest days

Having positive relationships increases your joy. The more time you spend with people who encourage you and bring out the best in you, the more you will also want to bring joy to other people.

How are your letters flowing? Most of the letters you've practiced have smoother lines rather than sharp edges. Remember to work on their rhythm and flow as you put your pen to paper.

Choose JOY
today, tomorrow,
and EVERY day

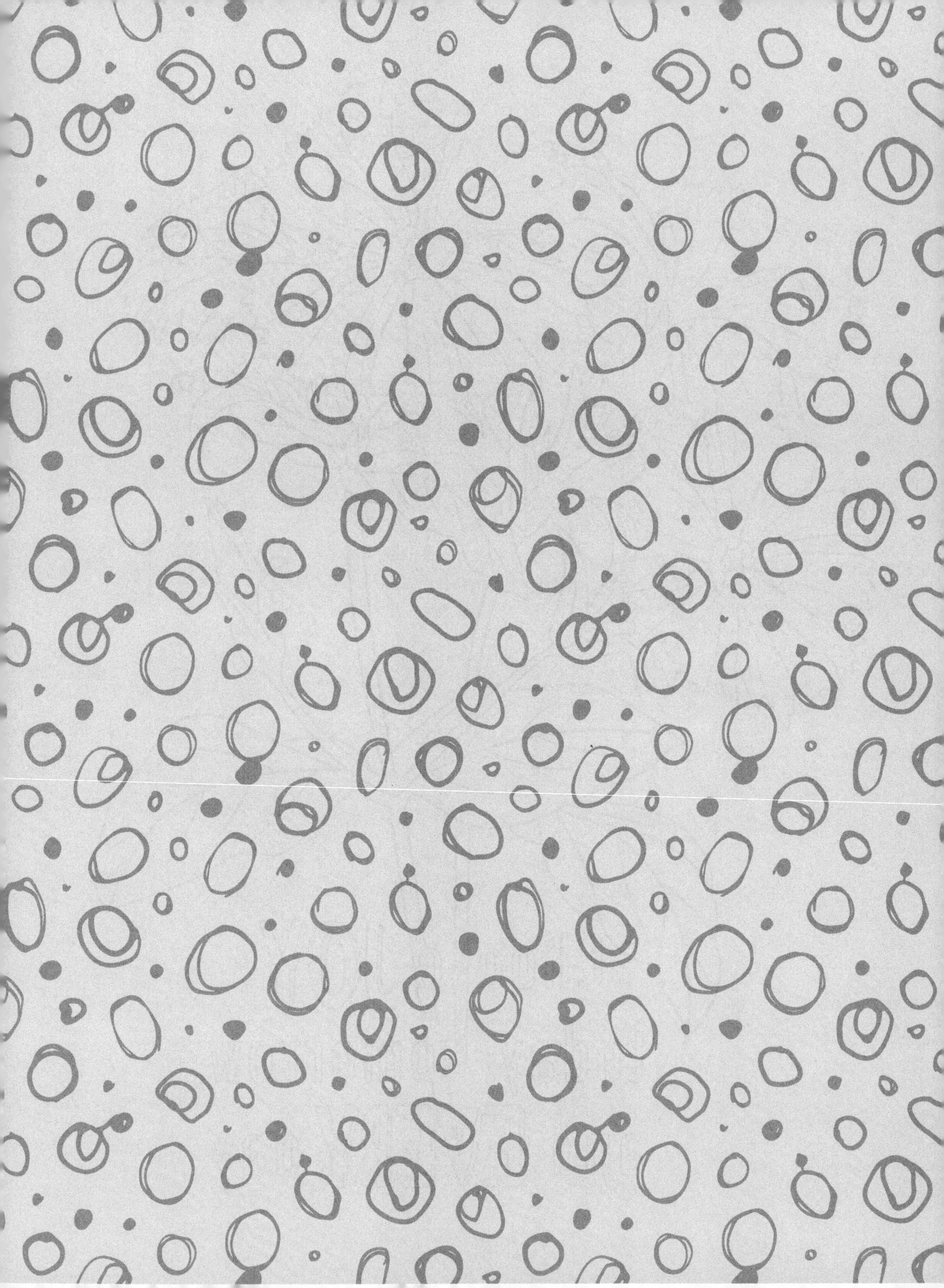

You're almost done with the lettering practice! For these last few letters, start thinking about how you can string these together to write the things that make you joyful.

v v

w w

x x

y y

z z

It's time for you to unleash your own creativity! With what you've learned in the previous exercises, write a letter to yourself about all the things that make you joyful. Use the lettering style you are most comfortable with.

Joy multiplies when it is shared

On this page, write a letter for someone in your life who helped you be more positive, someone who brings joy whenever you are together. Thank that person and encourage them to continue to be joyful.

Finally, think of or research your favorite quotes about joy and gratitude. Write the quotes that you relate to the most on this page. Writing down these quotes will also help you memorize, internalize, and meditate on what the message means.

Your JOY is the Spark that can light up the World

GRATITUDE POSTCARDS — color it

Developing a consistent gratitude practice can lead to a more joyful life. It focuses you on the good things that are happening and helps guide you to reframe your mindset when things don't go according to plan.

In the next exercise, you will be creating gratitude postcards. You've already written a letter to someone you're grateful for. Let's continue to write to more people in your life that you appreciate or people you want to encourage.

The boxes in this exercise are postcards. Write down your message for them, and then decorate the postcard however you like. You can even create your very own stamp.
Here's an example:

Dear friend,

Thank you for always sticking around. I appreciate all your effort. Continue to shine your light.

Love,

_____
[Your Name Here]

color it

Enjoy every moment

Here's another example to inspire you:

> Dear friend,
>
> I appreciate all the times you listen to me when I need someone to talk to. Thank you for being the shoulder I can lean on when I'm struggling. You are the best!
>
> Love,
>
> _____
> [Your Name Here]

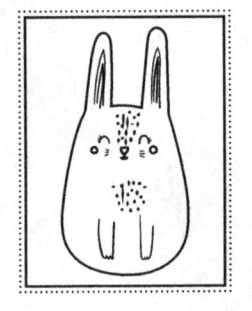

And don't forget to design the back of your postcard!

YOUR VIBE ATTRACTS YOUR TRIBE

Happiness is not out there

IT'S IN YOU

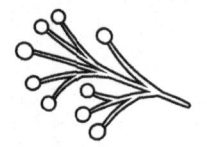

For this postcard, think of someone who helped you see the bright side of life and thank that person.

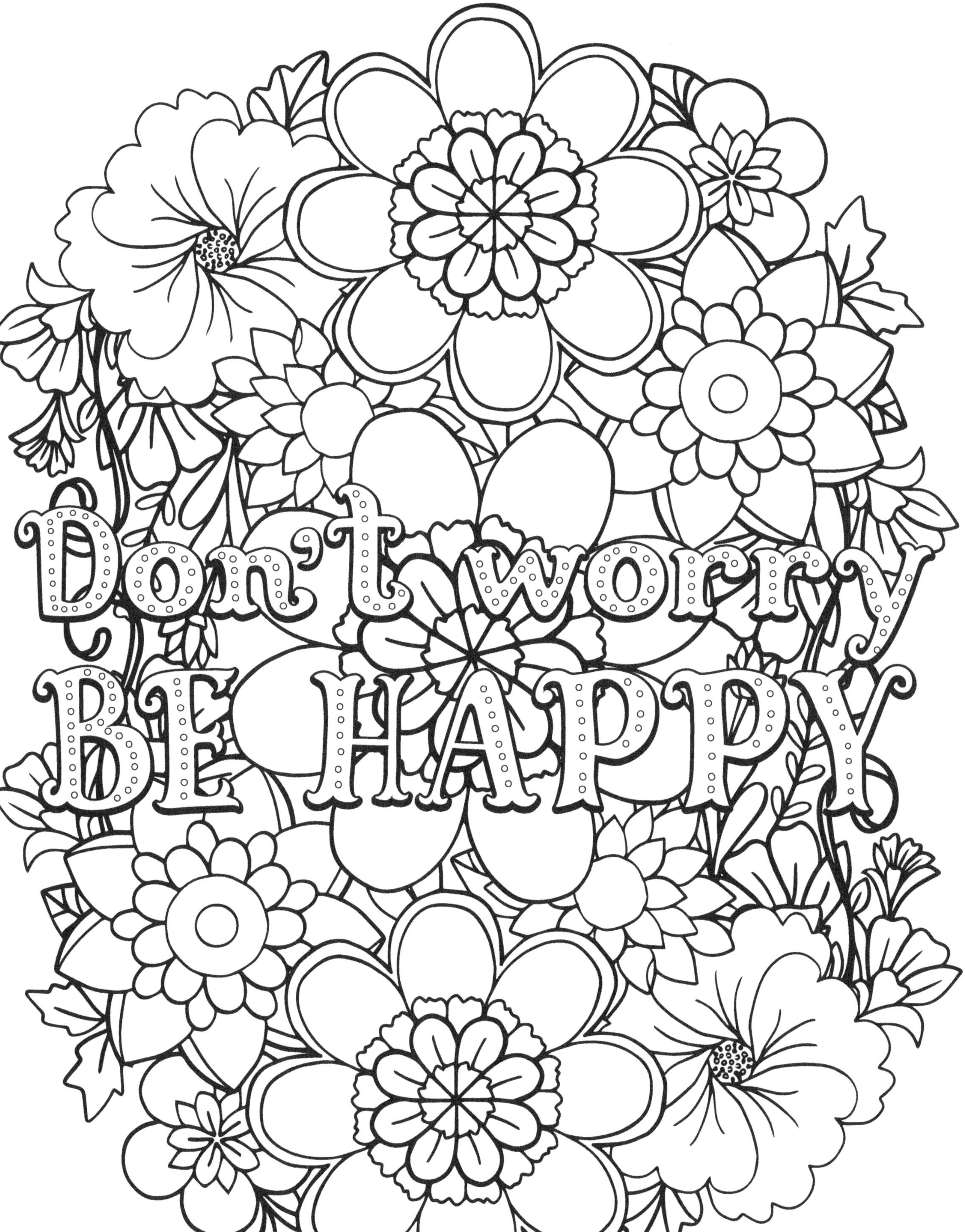
Don't worry
BE HAPPY

HAPPINESS IS A DIRECTION *not a place*

This time, thank someone you see every day and let them know you appreciate them.

Happiness depends upon ourselves

Having someone you enjoy spending time with is awesome!
Write your gratitude for them.

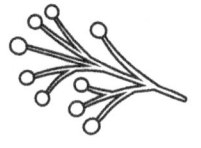

Don't forget to write a gratitude postcard for someone who recently taught you something new.

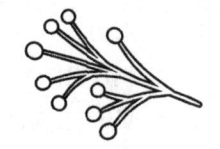

IF YOU WANT
TO BE HAPPY,
BE HAPPY

Have you thanked a public servant lately? Or someone who doesn't usually get noticed?

THE GREATEST WEALTH

is to live content with little

JOY

is the simplest form of gratitude

Write a gratitude postcard to a friend who lives far away but still keeps in contact with you!

WHEN ONE DOOR
OF HAPPINESS CLOSES,
ANOTHER OPENS

HAPPINESS is the higher level of success

Are there people in your life you haven't thanked yet?

When you focus on the goodness in your life, you create more of it

Expressing gratitude to people we love can help us live a more joyful life.

Writing short notes of appreciation and gratitude will help you develop a joyful mindset. If you want, you can create your own postcards on separate pieces of paper and actually give them to your loved ones and friends!

This postcard is for you. Remember to also be grateful for being who you are.

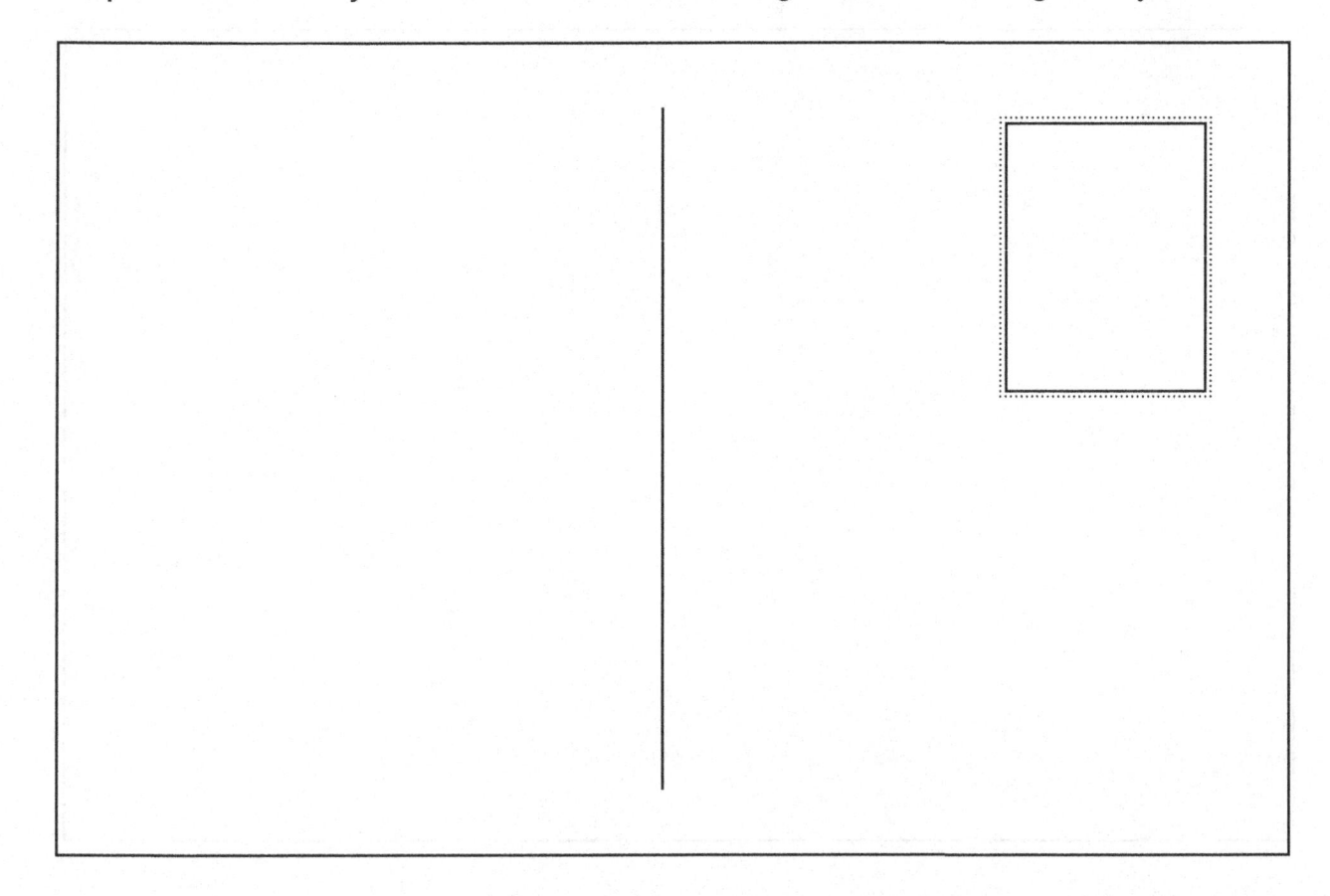

Joy is not in things it is in us

HAPPY WORD CLOUD

- color it

Let's do some introspection and reflection. It's important to know what makes you joyful. Getting to know how you respond to situations makes you more aware of which experiences you might want to get more of. In the next few pages, let's create your Happy Word Cloud.

What is a happy word cloud? It's exactly as the name suggests, a word cloud that encompasses things that make you happy. Let's start with a simple exercise:

Think of five things that made you happy today. It can be a gift you received, a person, a place, or even an experience. Write them down on the space below.

Things that made me happy today:

_____

_____

_____

_____

_____

Happiness held is the seed;
HAPPINESS SHARED IS THE FLOWER

Now place those five things inside this cloud.

Here's an example:

Ate some ice cream

Spent time with my friend

Had time to journal and reflect

Listened to my favorite music

Went out on a walk at the park

All warmed up and ready for more word clouds?

Let's repeat the exercise. Think of ten things that made you happy in the past week, and write them inside the cloud.

You can use different colored pens for your word cloud too!

THE SUNSHINE OF MY LIFE

Let's add more words to your word cloud!

Think about the things that make you happy about yourself. Do you like how spontaneous you are? Do you like how your hair looks? Write all the things you like about yourself inside the word cloud.

GRATITUDE
is a powerful catalyst for happiness

For this word cloud, think about what makes you happy in your surroundings. What do you like about where you live? Write all of it inside the word cloud.

Creating happy word clouds can be a good way to express your gratitude and joy. Each word cloud can be your reminder that life can be filled with many things that you are grateful for.

In the next few pages, think of the people who have influenced your life to become better and more joyful. Fill up word clouds about how they've helped you, what characteristics you most admire about them, and the emotions you feel when you are with them. You can also send them their own word clouds if you want.

Name:_____

FIND JOY
in everything you choose to do

**People who influence us sometimes don't even know how they've changed our lives.
This is your chance to think about how these people are valuable in your growth.**

Name:_____

GRATITUDE
turns what we have into enough

Keep noticing the things that you appreciate in people. Sharing these observations with them might also give them joy.

Name:_____

Name:_____

Being joyful is a mindset. And knowing why you are joyful is a focused awareness that can help you as you journey onward with your amazing life!

HAPPINESS IS NOT A GOAL. IT'S A BYPRODUCT

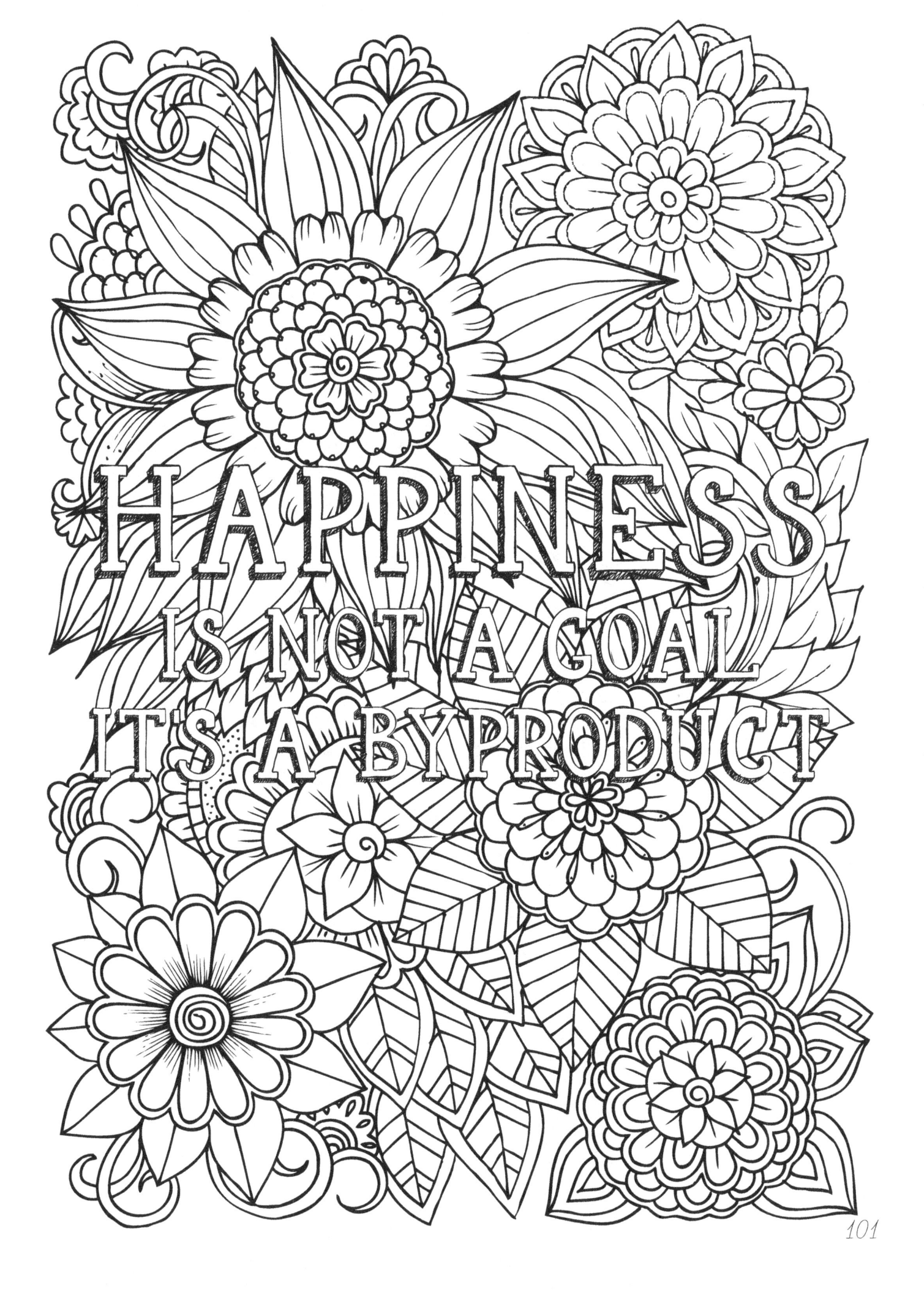

REFLECTION AND CELEBRATION — color it

Congratulations on finishing *Letters of Joy*! Every stroke you made in this book is an accomplishment that should be celebrated. Take a moment to reflect on the joy you've discovered in the art of lettering. Joy is not just a feeling; it's a practice and a way of seeing the world.

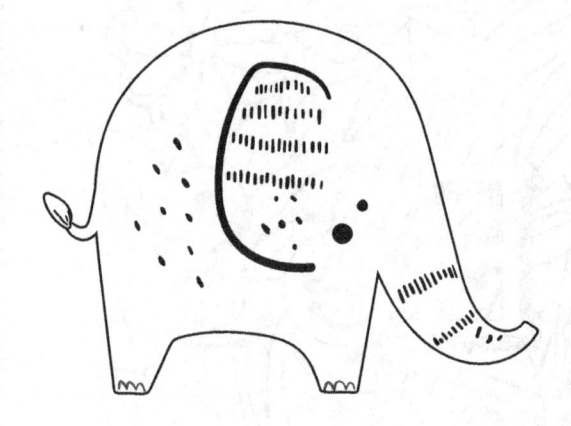

The joy you've found through these pages can be carried into every aspect of your life. Remember to be grateful and to find things that bring you joy wherever you are. The techniques and lettering styles you've learned can also help you express your joy creatively.

Keep creating and keep finding the beauty in the simple act of putting pen to paper. We hope your journey of gratefulness and lettering continues with endless joy and creativity.

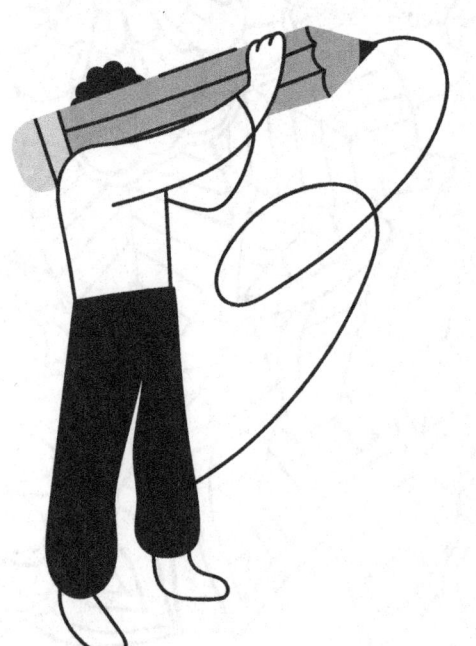

Thank you for sharing your journey of joy with us!

color it

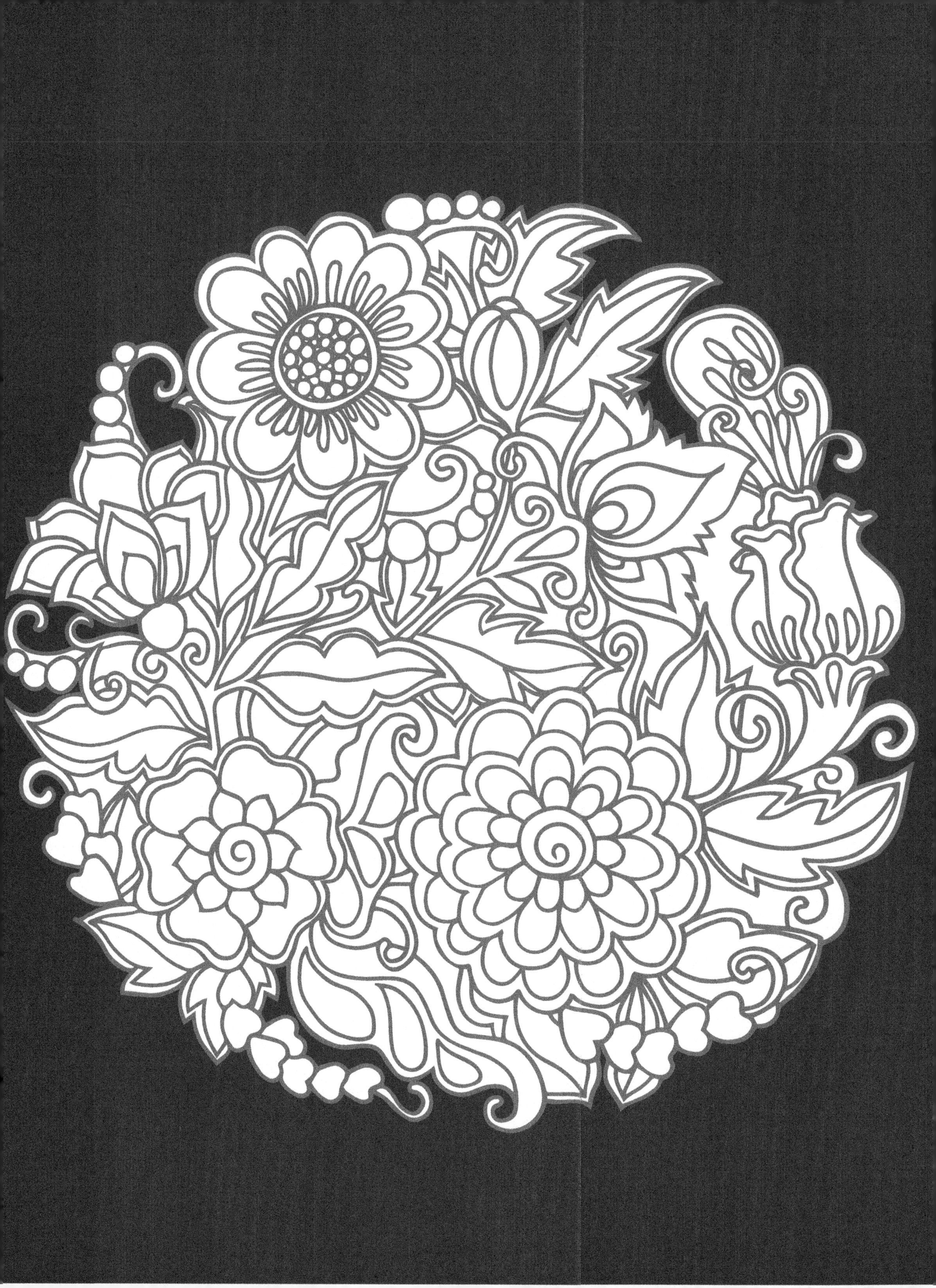

Made in the USA
Coppell, TX
22 February 2025